Tim Murphy

The Cacti Do Not Move

SurVision Books

First published in 2019 by
SurVision Books
Dublin, Ireland
Reggio di Calabria, Italy
www.survisionmagazine.com/books.htm

Copyright © Tim Murphy, 2019

Design © SurVision Books, 2019

ISBN: 978-1-912963-07-2

This book is in copyright. No part of this publication may be reproduced, stored in a retrieval system, or transmitted in any form or by any means without the prior permission in writing from the publisher.

Acknowledgements

Grateful acknowledgement is made to the editors of the journals in which a number of these poems, or versions thereof, originally appeared:

SurVision: "The Water Fire";
Otata: "Backing Vocal";
Otoliths: "Every Sunrise" and "The Cacti Do Not Move".

"Painted Canvases" is modelled after Noelle Kocot's poem, "Tongues", in *Humanity* (SurVision Books, 2018); "In a Mountain Dream" is modelled after the dream poems in Richard Hugo's collection, *31 Letters and 13 Dreams* (WW Norton & Company, 1977).

CONTENTS

The Water Fire	5
Spatula in Hand	6
Ostensibility	7
Backing Vocal	8
Painted Canvases	10
Urbanization	11
Every Sunrise	12
Route	13
Liberty Solitude	14
Poem for André Breton	15
The Cacti Do Not Move	16
Fear of Memory	17
In a Mountain Dream	18
Instrumental	19
Eating with Regret	20
The Tipping Point	21
Rock Leaves	22
Found	23
The Moat	24
Viscosity	25
Birds of Prey	26
Free on the Meadows	27
The Aurochs	28
Projection	30
Signs	31
New Colours	32
Autumn	33
Heal	34

"*Où la dialectique hégélienne ne fonctionne pas, il n'y a pas pour moi de pensée, pas d'espoir de vérité.*"

[*"Where the Hegelian dialectic does not function, there is for me no thought, no hope of truth."*]

—André Breton, *Entretiens* (1952)

The Water Fire

See the water fire,
Blue white yellow orange red,
It creates itself from nothing:
Alive it burn-flows and alive it flow-burns.

With wet dry wave-flames
And dry wet flame-waves
The water fire preserves itself:
It is a continuous affair.

The water fire is a part of time,
Part of desire passing through time
And of time passing through desire:
It is eternal.

The water fire quenches itself,
It is immune from any dearth of reality:
Creating, preserving, destroying,
Never and always at once.

Spatula in Hand

Spatula in hand she has no fear,
She is astride her dream;
In turpentine mornings
She would scutter and crawl for it.

In her colours there is fusion,
There is a coming together;
See the rhymes on canvas,
The half-rhymes on wood.

She steps back from the sound,
Her heart watches her eyes;
Each line gives birth to others,
The strokes never the same.

Oil moves to its own meter,
Gold flakes glint in the sunlight;
Her dream draws her along,
Spatula in hand she has no fear.

Ostensibility

The mind is a question,
A dream of unknowing.
You show me yours,
I show you mine.
We live like this for years,
Choices unmade,
Like life-paths at dusk,
Torn away from light.

We go underground to resist,
We tattoo vehicles coming out of nowhere,
We return and ask each other where we were;
We calculate an answer and divide it
By an archway to lesser decisions.

Change and desire keep intersecting
In the here and now,
As if the mind had been convinced,
In silent communion,
By the world.

There are ways back into the conundrum.
We can heed again
The howl of reason's age,
The clack of bitter love
Twisting and turning
In the magma of the night—
But what of the answer,
What of the knowing dream?

Backing Vocal

He was your common or garden convent wizard,
Always in a patchouli-coloured dream coat;
Dream sounds played on the radio
As he sang time's tune in the ears of the future
With all its memories;
And the old song,
All the time his elf would sing it—
Trailer for sale or rent,
Rooms to let, fifty cents—
Because of the poverty
And because of the cigarettes.

The shape of things to become
Changes with registers of time;
We did not know this then,
While our jaguar gods
Dreamed on and on;
And the old song,
The elf would really get into it—
No phone, no pool, no pets,
I ain't got no cigarettes—
And folded grief flags flew freely
In that convent.

Now, at the junction of it all,
I hear the battle horns
Sounding and circling,
I hear the drum beats
From the floating city;
And the old song,

I can still hear the elf singing it—
*I'm a man of means by no means,
King of the road*—
I throw my dark suit
Under a train.

Painted Canvases

A hint of ochre, like an infinity symbol,
Like a wide range of options.
Space is an age, time is a vessel.
Too joyful to consider, I have
Painted all the canvases, and yet. A masked
Compass shows the way. I measure
These things, height, depth, weight,
But I don't know where the razor
Is placed. It is the pain of confusion,
The sequence untitled and coming to fruition.
If I do not hesitate, it's so you'll renege.

Urbanization

The shapes moving in the morning mist
Are festivities without root or error;
Their ebbing pageantry fades all crests,
Pebbles all outbursts. Light stretches
Along the top of the underworld,
Forming an invisible mirror of time.
Many days cry out for recognition
But their voices cannot be heard.
Each and every glorious ruin stands alone,
Each and every pawnshop stands its ground;
Burnt skeletons witness the old myths
While welcoming new developments in brown,
And cobbled squares open wide their veins,
Invoking dahlia, daffodil, dandelion.

Every Sunrise

The sky is a parchment and yearning shuts down the sunset. Silken gusts push me down rural trails. I call to a woman in a disclosed mansion. She meets me on layers of moving grass and her hands are like bubbles in whitewater rapids. She says, "Clear warning chants ascend the cathedral bell rope yet the misguided flee the forest carriages and the hunted retreat into dry seas."

I meet the woman again while I am walking through a river valley. She appears on the riverbank and this time her hands are aflame. She holds her arms in the air, the flames starting from her wrists. She says, "When you walk in the fire tracks of the way, old age leaves the village like a wolf, insects seek rewards in the stillness, and bloodstones release blue numbers quietly."

The woman and I take to the byways and over time we get to know the land. At sad moments, we speak thoughts happily and a definite pattern is established. Sadness and happiness converge more and more frequently—and every sunrise we find objects already in our possession.

Route

Warred are we,
Between aqueducts we transport fire,
Between walls we design light.
We are attacked by something putrid,
Something bourgeois,
Something always wanting more.
Inert, we commission icons,
We assassinate at will;
Ever homeward bound,
Our writing is automatic.
Seven goats for the grey house ballet,
Eight horses for the deconstruction work,
A few pennies for burning our cars and shutting up—
There is a route
Out of here.

Liberty Solitude

Liberty Solitude testifies against late winter,
She offers a construction of lines and circles
As proof of prisons, of easy pieces.

Liberty Solitude spirals into control,
She becomes the vision of exhibition air.

Liberty Solitude walks on tracks of tomorrow,
She undergoes a ritual of lines and circles
To prepare for pain, for pure energy.

Liberty Solitude wears the world,
She runs into the silence of nature's sounds.

Liberty Solitude dances in trauma's arms,
She understands ideas of lines and circles
As portions of passion, of eternal peace.

Liberty Solitude carries an abacus,
She carries all that the planets carry.

Liberty Solitude ascends into the master dream,
She draws a composition of lines and circles
To perceive the pattern, the primal event.

Liberty Solitude sleeps on stories,
She consumes only her own drama.

Poem for André Breton

My spouses and lovers were long gone. I had relinquished all my hopes and all my fears. My children had become forest people. The idea of prey was to me anathema; all was shadow, all was spiral surrender. On the roads I toiled with and for love.

One day, for no apparent reason, I lost my memory. Naturally, and with wine and bread that never ended, I set out to find it. I had an idea of what I was looking for but no clear recollection. The idea ate the bread and drank the wine and tried to remember. It was all to no avail.

Appearing in dreams my idea's desire to remember revealed itself to be prey disguised as good disposition. I let everything go, once again, forever; and I began juxtaposing coincidences, right here, between these parallels.

The Cacti Do Not Move

A blue sepia shone somewhere in the monochrome of the apartment building, while mystic words about spiral life cycles seemed oblivious to the fact of our anaesthetic love heading for the rocks. I remember one of the green birds in your dream spoke of breaking the dawn and opening wide the gates of day, while my dream was of sacraments passing through trees and willow shavings hanging on wands as first snow offerings. It seems a spell was cast dialectically by the two dreams, at least that's the most plausible explanation for what happened in subsequent days and weeks. It was most likely this dialectic, for example, that prompted us to become our own winter secret. The dialectic theory would also explain the background cello sounds veering constantly into a ghost of a chance that either dream would recur. Ultimately, the whole situation, not least our spiralling arrangements in that apartment, took on a shade of tragedy blue. In fact, that was the blue sepia effect in the monochrome of the building. As regards the dissociated mantras, they have never been explained fully; perhaps a sacrament somehow passed through a day gate, or perhaps a life cycle melted into snow. What else is there to say? The death of our love, by convention I suppose, to nature belongs—but let's not forget, as a kind of addendum to that, that in our dream dialectic the dancers let go and then, suddenly, the cacti do not move and nor do we.

Fear of Memory

Fear of memory violence, violence of
Memory fear. Wounded rocks fall
From jagged cliffs. In the distance
I notice you, call to you. The waves
Are too loud until, when I call you again,
You hear me. Together, we lift
The ocean's skin, with memory,
With fear. The violence is close at hand.
In the space between you and I
Is time collapsed, time eclipsed.
I was there, too, with you.
Now it is time for us both
To come home: Come home, my love,
Home.

In a Mountain Dream

In a mountain dream
I am by the blue mountain.
It is morning and I feel the cool mountain wind.
I seek the river, but I am lost.
A woman walks down from the mountain.
I greet her and ask her where the river is.
Instead of answering she tells me her name is Nadja.
I am named after the book, she says.
In the distance I see the blue mountain
because now I am with Nadja by the river,
walking in sunlight, listening to the buzz of insects.
The past remains up for grabs, she says,
including more than the light, the water, and the matter.
Speaking of water, she adds, have you had enough
of the river? Yes, I say, and I explain
my feelings about mountains.
I understand, she says. Then I am with her
by the blue mountain again.
Now I know where the river is,
now the breeze is warm and gentle.
Nadja is trying to catch a butterfly with a net.
And something else, she shouts, laughing:
There are accidental encounters
tramped all over the rules of the game.

Instrumental

Sunday again.
A sombre sculpture moves
Through a highway underpass.
An empty studio is fractured
By a pious sunbeam.
A transit landscape shifts itself
To reveal a new absence,
A new marginalization.
The city prints
Another symbolic engine.
Sunday again!

Eating with Regret

Night begins, night ends.
Several ideas later, there is movement.
It feels like eating with regret.
Which images offer repose now?
The air conditioning that makes you feel
Less alone
Or
The velvet shimmer of magpie blue?

No, of course not, nothing like this.

Only a mounted canvas,
Completely blackened,
With the suggestion of taking a knife to it
Seething from itself—
And you, standing there,
For years and years,
Blade in hand.

Only this image offers repose.
Only in this image are you not a scapegoat.

After sharpening all the swords
You have put them away,
After re-shaping all the myths
You have put them away, too.
There is no heyday here,
No place to snap out of.

The Tipping Point

Take the days of supertramping in the lagered rain,
Of weighing each other's gold in blood, or take
The oak tree we understood, the hallucination
We made it become. Remember the portable
Passages of time, the prairie peninsulas
And the pagan ports, or when Hilma af Klint
Came to us in dreams, as the fruit of a long experience,
Showing us circles from the future . . .
                                  We are indeed all godlike,
But memory can become a satellite of betrayal,
And even if the treasure is always closer than we think,
And always waiting to be found, inhabited spirits
Cannot know this. Only the tipping point is known:
Hangmen rarely lie, and they do not avoid symmetry.

Rock Leaves

Despite the anarchy of possibility, and despite the fog of precision, withdrawn vessels continue to replace the high season with layers of language. In a lonely atlas the relevant moments of decline are scattered, and contrary to what was assumed, the water is not opaque, the bridge is not wide.

These are torchlit times, layers of language mingle with different levels of light, and the seasonal flux is still in force. Forest earth evokes future days. A voice does sing but the words are not clear, not even the language is clear.

A lone cloud appears over the bridge. The moon is absent. Bright words are hunted in a low ravine while trees escape into secret valleys. A chaotic mist whispers loudly but the breeze on the water makes no sound and the rock leaves hardly rustle at all.

Found

For Gerard Staunton

One day it will be there, easy to find.

Don't expect any kind of fanfare.

There will be no firebird chorus
In silver-tint wind.

One day it appears, or you create it,
Or it creates you or itself
By appearing,
Or by being created by you.

Again: don't expect any kind of fanfare,
It will simply be there, easy to find.

The Moat

Logic's rain falls,
Naked to the touch.
The annual mirrors carry valuable cargo
While the redbrick moon and the hummingbirds
Remain silent.

Jupiter and Venus share a joke
By the high-rise vegetation,
Something about a double agency bind—
The fairy lights on the bridge
Are broken but alive.

Saturn watches the rhythm
Of the vaulting night,
He stretches and brushes his teeth.
The next two waves
Will make all the difference.

Viscosity

The oils await a gilded guideline,
A canvas mark to believe in;
I wonder what is required
For things to continue like this.

The figure inspires like muslin
Primed with chalk;
The petal eyes, the stem neck,
The absence of age.

Nature is singing again,
There are divine horses on the run;
It is timely, this space deficit,
This nostalgia in an infinite loop.

There is talk on the ragwort ridge,
Gossip about the round flower-heads;
But it is merely a dawn defect,
Gauze from the other side.

Calm is restored
With new frames, with pinked skin;
It seems nothing is required
For things to continue like this.

Birds of Prey

Night's hard shoulder. Dazed, we act out,
Into a composition of parody and pain.
Notice what we've compressed.
Anger at the recurrence,
The detour of a concept.

We are in a portrait of the present,
Made warm by humanity
And dispersed like a sieve of light.

Humming along nicely, we each become
A bird of prey, you a black eagle,
I a western osprey.

Withdrawn thus by waking reality
City streets conduct us like copper wire,
Yet we block ourselves at every turn.
What's with that?

A shadow-check in the sun,
A spoken word in the thicket,
Before we know what's happening,
We each emerge with our own gold.
The old dispensation is rejected.

Free on the Meadows

The empty congestion of the future suggests happenings will replace galleries sooner rather than later. One can sense the impending pattern of substitution by surveying the situation retrospectively: the grey history of curation is inlaid with unsavoury exchequered designs; collectives act like voyeurs from the invisible world; and the only available performance artists are ghost-codes. There are other hints, too: large-boned canvases lie static in the streets; permission is being sought to frame the sky for a month; and the eye spots of starfish, more rosemary than bergamot, somewhere comprise an exhibition. Ultimately, among the installations making demands in the flames, it's impossible to find even one image submerged in blood. In contrast, the happenings run free on the meadows, crying and laughing in the face of all the emptiness, all the congestion.

The Aurochs

For Tinna Ingvarsdóttir

Every week at a certain hour
On a certain day
I float in a sea of floating women.

The sea is clear—
In the shallow parts
You can see
Right through the water—
And every week at the same hour
On the same day,
As I float in this clear sea,
I paint universal circles,
Universal doorways:
I paint mandalas.

All the women are painting, too,
Painting as they float in the clear sea.
They paint maps with shorelines,
They paint territories with vegetation,
They paint tigers, angels and graves:
They paint the windows of their pain.

Every week at the same hour
On the same day,
When we float and paint in the clear sea,
These women and I,

We are all copying the pictures
Of the wild cattle on old cave walls;
We are all painting the bison, the wild bulls,
We are all painting the aurochs.

We paint for luck in the hunt,
We paint to cope with our trauma,
We paint our ritual need.

We paint windows of pain and we paint mandalas—
We paint the aurochs.

Projection

I have labyrinth intuition worship,
Vital monster regeneration,
And action symphony legacies;
You have vinyl destiny planets,
Congealed brownstone seas,
And original excursus devotion.

We can turn down the music
And cook up a still life
With an octopus and galloping red horses,
We can plan for a citizens' banquet
As part of a formula for spring,
There can be grand glove gestures
And there can be fire falling free.

Call it the decay of an elementary dream
Or call it a quiet watershed,
But killing ghosts are weaving through the dream canals
And microdot marriages are calling out
For some mean time, some screen time,
Some me time and some manic-phase time . . .
Oh yes, believe it, this fantasia is real.

Signs

The radiant future dies slowly,
The signs of the process are hard to miss.
Its system of content moderation collapses first,
Then the age of its slavery is exposed as illusion
And selected sublimations gradually come back to life.
Soon islands start to surface in seas of grey graffiti,
Backstreet baptisms start to peter out,
And every single screen explodes.
Finally, in the native rodeo metropolis,
Near the ruptured mannequin barriers,
A lone eagle always crashes and—
Slowly, very slowly—
Burns.

New Colours

New colours of death
Await us all.
I tell you this
Not to hurt you
But rather to help you—
For what more
Can we wish for
Than journeys with directions
Sharply defined?
What are the alternatives?
Going for lunch?
Going on holiday?
Going on a hiatus?
Maybe a secret noise
Is needed,
Or maybe the grief itself
Is simply dead.
Anyway,
Believe me,
The afterlife
Is not far worse.

Autumn

At the night gate the sense
Of contrasting patterns.

The moment when I decide to stay
Eludes me.

The heart is an answer,
Like a dead flower with its poetry
Tilting toward the edge of something spare,
Something not urban or even complex.

I tell you again I love you—
You reply
With an argument
From tradition.

The patterns merge
Without synthesizing,
Marking a point in space
That hums before disappearing.

Heal

This ink runs its course,
As do wind and stone—
Mark the cave,
Scratch the wall.

Fight for your lifeline,
For your hopeful fear;
Fight for it, win it,
Be with it, run with it.

This energy finds light,
As do sound and space—
Paint the blue sky,
Draw the silent island.

Breach the surface,
The template of harmony;
Heal your heart,
Wake your sleeping dream.

More poetry published by SurVision Books
(available to order via http://survisionmagazine.com/books.htm)

Noelle Kocot. *Humanity*
(New Poetics: USA)
ISBN 978-1-9995903-0-7

Ciaran O'Driscoll. *The Speaking Trees*
(New Poetics: Ireland)
ISBN 978-1-9995903-1-4

Helen Ivory. *Maps of the Abandoned City*
(New Poetics: England)
ISBN 978-1-912963-04-1

Elin O'Hara Slavick. *Cameramouth*
(New Poetics: USA)
ISBN 978-1-9995903-4-5

John W. Sexton. *Inverted Night*
(New Poetics: Ireland)
ISBN 978-1-912963-05-8

Afric McGlinchey. *Invisible Insane*
(New Poetics: Ireland)
ISBN 978-1-9995903-3-8

George Kalamaras. *That Moment of Wept*
ISBN 978-1-9995903-7-6

Anton Yakovlev. *Chronos Dines Alone*
(Winner of James Tate Poetry Prize 2018)
ISBN 978-1-912963-01-0

Bob Lucky. *Conversation Starters in a Language No One Speaks*
(Winner of James Tate Poetry Prize 2018)
ISBN 978-1-912963-00-3

Christopher Prewitt. *Paradise Hammer*
(Winner of James Tate Poetry Prize 2018)
ISBN 978-1-9995903-9-0

Mikko Harvey & Jake Bauer. *Idaho Falls*
(Winner of James Tate Poetry Prize 2018)
ISBN 978-1-912963-02-7

Anatoly Kudryavitsky. *Stowaway*
(New Poetics: Ireland)
ISBN 978-1-9995903-2-1

Maria Grazia Calandrone. *Fossils*
Translated from Italian
(New Poetics: Italy)
ISBN 978-1-9995903-6-9

Sergey Biryukov. *Transformations*
Translated from Russian
(New Poetics: Russia)
ISBN 978-1-9995903-5-2

Alexander Korotko. *Irrazionalismo*
Translated from Russian
(New Poetics: Ukraine)
ISBN 978-1-912963-06-5

Anton G. Leitner. *Selected Poems 1981–2015*
Translated from German
ISBN 978-1-9995903-8-3

www.ingramcontent.com/pod-product-compliance
Lightning Source LLC
Chambersburg PA
CBHW061313040426
42444CB00010B/2621